How I Feel About My School

A Story to Identify and Reflect on Children's Emotions

ANITA LEHMANN

ILLUSTRATED BY KARIN EKLUND

Advised by Professor Claire Hughes,
Dr Elian Fink and the Ready or Not Study Team

Routledge
Taylor & Francis Group
LONDON AND NEW YORK

Designed cover image: Illustration by Karin Eklund

First published 2025
by Routledge
4 Park Square, Milton Park, Abingdon, Oxon OX14 4RN

and by Routledge
605 Third Avenue, New York, NY 10158

Routledge is an imprint of the Taylor & Francis Group, an informa business

British Library Cataloguing-in-Publication Data
A catalogue record for this book is available from the British Library

Library of Congress Cataloging-in-Publication Data
Names: Lehmann, Anita, author. | Eklund, Karin (Karin Elisabeth), illustrator.
Title: How I feel about my school : a story to identify and reflect on children's emotions / Anita Lehmann ; illustrated by Karin Eklund.
Description: Abingdon, Oxon ; New York, NY : : Routledge, 2025.
Identifiers: LCCN 2024037269 (print) | LCCN 2024037270 (ebook) | ISBN 9781032880846 (paperback) | ISBN 9781003536888 (ebook)
Subjects: LCSH: School day—Juvenile literature. | Neurodivergent children—Juvenile literature.
Classification: LCC LB1556 .L45 2025 (print) | LCC LB1556 (ebook) | DDC 372.21—dc23/eng/20240916
LC record available at https://lccn.loc.gov/2024037269
LC ebook record available at https://lccn.loc.gov/2024037270

ISBN: 978-1-032-88084-6 (pbk)
ISBN: 978-1-003-53688-8 (ebk)

DOI: 10.4324/9781003536888

Typeset in VAG Rounded Std
by Apex CoVantage, LLC

Acknowledgements

Thanks to all parents and children who took part in the Ready or Not Study, and the full research team, including *Dr Caoimhe Dempsey* at the Economic and Social Research Institute in Dublin, Ireland, *Dr Laura Katus* at the University of Greenwich, and a large and lovely team of PhD students and research assistants. Thanks also to *Dr Adrian Cheng* and the WEMP Foundation for supporting a Hong Kong based 'sister' Ready or Not Study, and to *Professor Tamsin Ford*, who developed the child questionnaire "How I Feel About My School". For more information, see: http://medicine.exeter.ac.uk/phss/research/chyme/hifams/. Finally, we are grateful to *Allie Mason*, who guided us in representing neurodiversity.

Here are Hanna, Jessie, Akira, and Hassan.

Let's join them for a day at school.

It's drop-off time.
Jessie bounces, Akira tugs,
Hassan runs, and Hanna hugs.

How are they feeling right now?

It's show-and-tell time.
Hassan wriggles, Jessie drums, Hanna listens, Akira hums.

Is it a bit loud for him?

What helps you when it all gets too much?

It's break time! Everyone is out to play.

Akira watches, Hassan calls,
Jessie cartwheels, Hanna . . . falls!

Ouch!

Has someone seen what happened?

What makes you feel better when you're hurt?

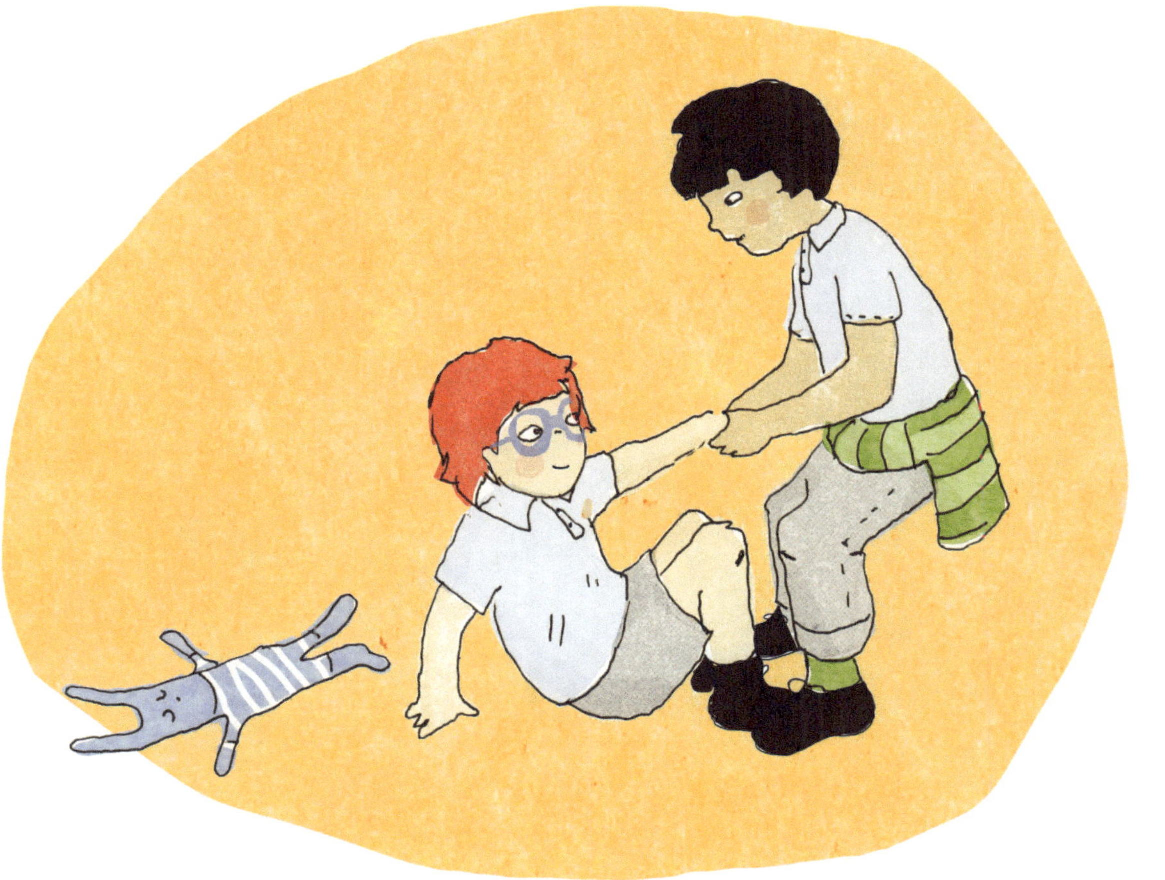

It's lunch time.

Akira munches,
Hanna snacks,
Hassan pushes in,
Jessie pushes back.

Uh oh.
What do you think
might happen next?

What are Jessie and Hassan saying to each other?

It's quiet time in the classroom.

Akira and Hanna
build a town,
Hassan draws,
and Jessie
scowls.

Her pencils keep breaking.

What helps you when you get frustrated?

It's pick-up time.

Hassan hugs, Akira waves,
Jessie skips, and Hanna smiles.

How did they
feel at school today?

Now it's your turn! Let's talk about YOUR day at school.

How do you feel when you think about:

drop-off time

quiet class time

active class time

lunch time

break time

your friends?

So many words to say how we feel!

Here are just a few:

surprised

sad

excited

worried

overwhelmed

sorry

upset

angry

connected

joyful
proud
thankful
tired
frustrated
creative
keen
happy

The book follows four different characters who have different experiences across the day. Children may like to focus on one character at a time, to consider how and why their feelings change as the day unfolds. The book can also be read across different settings (e.g., group discussions or one-to-one reading) or as a straightforward picture book with interactive elements that enable children to pitch in. Connecting the events in the story to those in children's own life will help build their empathy and ability to "stand in others' shoes". We hope that the emotions vocabulary chart at the end of the book helps make sharing feelings a routine part of children's life, as regular conversations about feelings are a great way of helping children understand their own and others' emotions.

We hope that this book is useful to you in encouraging the young child(ren) in your life – at home or in the classroom – to reflect on their daily experiences at school. Alongside the easy-to-spot accidents and upsets, the book includes joyful moments and acts of kindness. While it's good to remember that all feelings are important, helping children to notice these positive moments will help build their social confidence.

Why Did We Write This Book?

The idea for this book came from a recent ESRC-funded study led by Professor Claire Hughes. This study involved two waves of interviews with 200+ children and their parents – in Reception and again in Year 1. The results showed that children's and parents' responses to the "How I Feel About My School" questionnaire were quite different in Reception but more similar in Year 1. Moreover, how parents responded in Year 1 was often similar to their children's responses in Reception, indicating that it can take parents almost a year to tune into their child's experiences at school. One simple reason for this is that it can be very difficult to get children to say anything about their school day. Parents may also get a misleading picture if children are motivated to talk about their school day when something has upset them but less likely to talk about their more positive day-to-day experiences.

The study also showed that individual differences in how children feel at school in Reception year are important, as they predict later contrasts in both prosocial acts (e.g., sharing, helping, comforting) and children's confidence in their cognitive abilities. As a problem shared is a problem halved, we hope that this book will be useful for teachers and parents who'd like to talk about building children's emotional vocabularies and their understanding of how different situations can make different people happy or sad and how small acts of kindness can make a big difference!

Anita Lehmann is a versatile, award-winning author of fiction and non-fiction for both children and adults. Born and raised in Bern, Switzerland, and with an MA in economic and social history from the University of Geneva, Anita has lived, studied, and worked in many different places before making Cambridge, UK, home for herself and her family. She usually writes in a shed at the back of her garden, drinking English tea and missing Swiss chocolate, with her black spaniel snoring at her feet.

Karin Eklund is an artist and illustrator living and working in Cambridge, UK. Her studio is in Milton Country Park, where she works daily. Her main commissions are for children's books, but she also works with academic book titles, museum educational material, and collaborations with researchers.

Professor Claire Hughes is a developmental psychologist at the University of Cambridge, UK, where she is a Fellow at Newnham College and Deputy Head at the Psychology Department. She was the lead researcher on the ESRC-funded Ready or Not study, which aimed to bring together different viewpoints on school readiness and highlighted the difficulties that many parents face in getting a clear picture of their young child's life at school.

Dr Elian Fink is based at the School of Psychology, University of Sussex, UK. Her work focusses on how best to support children's social skills and peer relationships at the transition to school and was a co-investigator of the ESRC-funded Ready or Not study, alongside *Dr Rory Devine* at the University of Birmingham and *Dr Hana D'Souza* at Cardiff University.